Speaking in Social Contexts

Speaking in Social Contexts

Communication for Life and Study in the U.S.

Robyn Brinks Lockwood
Stanford University

ANN ARBOR
UNIVERSITY OF MICHIGAN PRESS

Copyright © by Robyn Brinks Lockwood, 2018
All rights reserved
Published in the United States of America
The University of Michigan Press
Manufactured in the United States of America

♾ Printed on acid-free paper

ISBN-13: 978-0-472-03716-2 (paper)
ISBN-13: 978-0-472-12446-6 (ebook)

2021   2020   2019   2018   4   3   2   1

Acknowledgments

The author would like to thank the following people:

- Editor extraordinaire, Kelly Sippell, for her support and expertise.

- Parents, Virgil and June Brinks, for their unfailing belief in education and family.

- Husband, John Lockwood, for his patience as the dining room table was covered by page proofs and corpus search results.

- Family members, Tim, Darrin, and Nathan, for unintentionally providing me with examples of how people really talk.

- The manuscript reviewers, for their willingness to help and share their experience to make this a better book.

  and

- The countless students who have taken my speaking courses, for their hard work and dedication to wanting to be the best English speakers they can be.

Contents

Introduction

Over the years, I've traveled domestically (around the United States) and internationally. My international travel, for business and pleasure, has taken me both to places where I knew a little bit of the language and to places where I didn't speak the language at all. In both situations, I've been in a variety of contexts and settings—social, academic, and professional—with a variety of people of different ages, genders, and statuses at different times and locations. I noticed that three factors seemed to impact the interaction: word choice, voice, and non-verbal communication. In terms of word choice, there are certain words or phrases to use to use to serve particular words or functions. For example, *To me . . .* is often a phrase used to let someone know an opinion will follow. In thinking about the influence of voice, a speaker needs to consider tone (emotion), intonation, stress (syllable and word), volume, and speed (how fast or slowly something is said). To give an example, someone who says, *I'm not angry at YOU*, is still angry but is emphasizing that they are not angry with me (as opposed to someone else). Last, non-verbal language—such as body language, facial expression, gestures, posture, or eye contact—can also play a role, possibly enhancing, detracting from, or replacing word choice or voice cues.

For each possible combination of context, I noticed how interaction shifts. For example, I might talk to a person of the opposite sex differently at work than I would at a social dinner. Or, I might be talking to the exact same person, say my colleague, but we would talk about different things depending on where we were or what time of day it was. Think about a phrase such as *How are you?* Said woman to woman, it can be a simple inquiry. Said man to woman, it can take on a whole new meaning, especially when combined with non-verbal language and tone or when spoken in class versus spoken at a party. I realized my students needed to be aware of factors such as gender, time, location, status, relationship, and content.

Despite all the differences and contexts, there were many patterns that began to emerge as I studied the language. As someone who was very shy and reserved, I began to notice these patterns and found they could help me "survive" any interaction. To illustrate, I noticed that when someone greets someone in English with *How are you?* the answer is almost always positive (*I'm good*); when someone might answer with a negative response is usually based on the relationship—someone who knows the other person very well might answer more truthfully with *Not so good*. Knowing that there are common responses and patterns to various greetings and closings can help students fear interaction less. There are tips that help them "predict" to some degree what might happen.

Also, when I traveled to a place where I knew a little of the language, I noticed how quickly I was overwhelmed. The language I heard "in real life" didn't sound anything like it sounded in my classroom or in the textbooks from which I had studied. When I began teaching, I noticed this was also true for my students who had studied English for many years but who, after arriving in the United States, quickly realized that what they had learned as English was not what they heard now. The English taught in textbooks is sometimes very prescriptive. It is what we are supposed to say; however, it rarely is what we really do say. To give an example, students often learn this dialogue:

Hello. How are you?

I am well. Thank you. And you?

I can't think of the last time I said *And you?* First, most Americans* don't speak grammatically. Rather than saying *I am well*, they say *I'm good*. International students need to be prepared for that contracted, ungrammatical response. And then they need to be ready for the question that will not be *And you?* Rather, it'll be *You? How 'bout you?* or *How're you?* Therefore, it was important for me to provide a book that teaches the language prescriptively as well as descriptively (letting

---

*We use the term *Americans* in this book to refer to people in North America and primarily those in the United States (although we know people from Central and South America are also Americans).

students review that foundational language and then add the more realistic English they will hear). Then students need to move beyond the book and actually use the language.

This text was written for students who want to live, study, and/or work in an English-speaking setting or are already doing so. It consists of 10 units meant to help students survive interactional English in a variety of social, academic, and professional settings. The text provides language to use for a variety of functions: greetings, closings, introductions, opinions, agreement, disagreement, phone use, assistance, advice, excuses, invitations, compliments, complaints, congratulations, condolences, and small talk. The content encourages students to think beyond just using the "right" words. It encourages them to think about pronunciation, intonation, and tone—how things sound. It's not what a person says, but how they said it. Just because someone uses exactly the right words to apologize or greet someone, if the tone or intonation is "off," then the interaction can be disastrous. Students need to be able to recognize tone and then use it. They also need to consider non-verbal language that can accompany the words and tone.

These materials have been developed from 10 years of teaching a class called Interacting in English at Stanford University that is designed to help students be able to talk and work with Americans while they are living, studying, and working in the United States. Content is drawn from observations, corpus collections, and data collection my students and I have collected from homework assignments in class.

The text can be used as the main text or a supplemental text in speaking or culture courses or as part of integrated listening/speaking classes. The units can easily be used sequentially, but it need not be. One unit does not need to be finished before another, so teachers can pick and choose based on student needs. However, beginning with Unit 1 is recommended since greetings typically begin most English interactions.

Each unit consists of discussion starters, language lessons, practice activities, contact exercises, and analysis activities.

• **Discussion Starter**: These questions are designed to get students thinking about the material covered in the unit. The questions might ask about their personal experiences or observations, ask them to consider their native languages or cultures, or ask them to guess what they might see or hear "in real life." The idea is to focus them on the function as well as the culture and other factors that might affect an interaction.

• **Language Lesson:** The language lessons will include foundational information such as common expressions students might hear (corpus-informed or compiled from data collection), formal versus informal phrasing, a comparison of what they probably learned and what is more likely, strategies to use, common responses, and important things to notice. Some Language Lessons include information about pronunciation to guide students on some key ways that these phrases may sound. The Appendix can be used as a quick reference. No attempt is made here to address the teaching of pronunciation, just to make students aware of how the way something is said can affect meaning.

• **Practice Activity**: Each unit has several practice activities that help students apply what they have learned. Activities include situational analyses, situational simulations, role-plays, and those that improve pronunciation or phrasing. Many practice activities are designed for pair or small group work, but instructors can vary this or even ask students to work individually before comparing answers.

• **Get Acquainted**: Each unit has at least one contact activity so students have to use the language they have learned and hear the way that native speakers use the language. Contact activities include data collection, surveys, interviews, and observations.

• **Analysis Activities:** Each Get Acquainted activity gives students the chance to compare their "data" with others to learn what English is being used and determine patterns to the responses. The activities help them to begin to notice factors such as gender—that women might answer differently than men—or status— that someone might use different language based on their position. By completing these activities, students can fear English less and grow their confidence so that they use the language and become active participants on and off campus.

Unit 1

Greetings, Goodbyes, and Introductions

Part 1: Greetings and Goodbyes

Discussion Starter

- How do you greet people when you are in your home country?

- How common is it to talk to a stranger in your home country? What are the benefits and drawbacks to talking to someone you don't know?

- Share a story of a time when you met a native English speaker. How did you introduce yourself or how were you introduced?

Language Lesson: Greetings

What are some greetings you are familiar with?

Some of these greetings might be more familiar to you than others.

Good morning/Good afternoon/Good evening.

Hi/Hey/Hello.

What's up/What's going on/What's happening/What's new?

How are you/How are you doing/How have you been?

Good to see you/Nice to see you.

Long time, no see.

Pronunciation Note: No matter how formal the greeting looks, most greetings sound more casual or informal. For example: Good morning will sound more like *G-mornin'* or *Mornin'*. Native speakers might also link or shorten phrases. *What's up* might sound like *'Tsup?* and the word *you* will likely sound like *ya*.

Language Lesson: Goodbyes (or Closings)

In American* culture, native speakers do not typically end a conversation with the word *goodbye*. There is usually a **pre-goodbye** before the actual word *goodbye*. Why? It is expected—a "social contract" of sorts. It avoids abruptness and the possibility of sounding unfriendly. This pre-goodbye might be something as simple as the words *Okay* or *So*. A sample pre-goodbye might be *Well, I'm afraid I have to be going* or *I've gotta be going*. The other person will then respond with a pre-goodbye, such as *Me, too,* before either person says *goodbye* or *bye*.

Other pre-goodbyes:

It's been a pleasure.

It's been great.

Okay, thanks (in phone calls or after office hours).

It was nice/good/great to see you.

It's getting late.

Thanks or coming (social or professional party or meeting).

We'll have to get together sometime.

I have got to go/run.

I have to be going.

I better get going.

Then you add a closing after the pre-goodbye:

See you later.

See you tomorrow.

Goodbye or Goodnight.

Have a good [weekend].

Talk to you later.

Bye.

Take it easy.

So long.

Have a good one.

*We use the term *Americans* in this book to refer to people in North America and primarily those in the United States (although we know that people from Central and South America are also Americans).

Pronunciation Note: **Tone** expresses a speaker's attitude or emotion. It conveys meaning beyond the words that are chosen. In writing, tone is often conveyed through word choice. With speaking, tone is conveyed through the sound of your voice. You might hear someone say, "It's not what she said, it's how she said it." This means that the person likely said the "right" words, but the tone didn't match. You can say *It was great to see you,* but if you say it in a way that makes you sound sad or angry, then the person will not believe that you truly thought it was good to see them.

PRACTICE 1: FORMALITY

Categorize the greetings and goodbyes into those that you think are more formal and those that are more informal.

Formal	Informal
Greetings	
Goodbyes	

PRACTICE 2: PRONUNCIATION

Work with a partner. Write how you think each greeting and goodbye (or closing) <u>sounds</u> when delivered by a native speaker. When responding, consider whether you hear every syllable and letter and what the prominent or stressed word or syllable is.

1. Hello: _____

2. Good to see you: _____

3. How are you? _____

4. How have you been? _____

5. What's up? _____

6. I have to be going: _____

7. It was nice to see you: _____

8. I got to go: _____

9. Goodbye: _____

10. See you/See you later: _____

PRACTICE 3: RESPONSES

Work with a partner. List a common response to each greeting or goodbye (closing). Guess if you're not sure.

Greeting	Common Response
Good morning/Good afternoon/Good evening.	
Hi/Hey/Hello.	
Hi/Hey/Hello, [NAME]	
How are you?/How are you doing?/How have you been?	
Good to see you/Nice to see you.	
Long time, no see.	
I have to go/run.	
It's been great.	
Thanks.	
It was nice to see you.	
It's getting late.	
Thanks for coming.	
Maybe we could get together sometime.	

Greeting	Common Response
Later.	
Have a good weekend.	
See you later.	
Bye.	
Take it easy.	

Get Acquainted

Greet five people. Complete the chart with the greeting you used, the response you heard, and a short note about the interaction (person/relationship to you, age, gender, status, time, location, content, context). Be prepared to share your notes in class. An example has been done for you.

Greeting	Response	Notes
Hey.	Hey.	Classmate in my chemistry class at 9:30 AM.

PRACTICE 4: ANALYSIS

Work with a group. Compare your Get Acquainted charts and answer these questions.

1. Were the responses ones you expected? Why or why not? Did you hear any words/phrases you had never heard before? Did you know what they meant?

2. In many cases, English is formulaic. You can predict what a person will say and prepare some phrases that are easy for you to remember and pronounce. Do you see any patterns to the greetings and responses?

3. What notes do you have about each interaction in Column 3? Did these affect the response? Did this affect the patterns you noticed? For example, did status or relationship affect your answers? Would a professor answer the same way as one of your classmates?

Part 2: Making Introductions

Discussion Starter

- When you meet someone new, do you use handshakes or some other non-verbal language to accompany the greeting?

- What titles (if any) do you use?

- In your home country, how do you address teachers? How do teachers address students? How is this the same or different from what you will see at English-speaking universities?

Language Lesson: Introductions

A formal introduction generally consists of two parts:

1. providing names

2. giving some information about the people

This may be very different from what you may have learned before.

What You Learned	What Is More Common
Joon, I would like to introduce you to my friend, Carlita.	Joon, this is Carlita. Carlita, Joon. Joon. Carlita. Carlita and I met in Chem Lab.

When it comes to giving information about people, titles or honorifics are often used. However, in many American settings, **titles** or **honorifics** are not used as often as you may think. At a university, especially the graduate level, students call teachers by their first names. Honorifics are used sometimes for people you are meeting the first time, in email or written correspondence, or out of respect. It is likely that people may "correct" you or let you know it is okay to call them by their first name if you use an honorific.

Example: at a Chemistry Department meeting between TAs and professors:

> *Student*: Dr. Smith, I'm the TA for Chem 101.
>
> *Dr. Smith*: Nice to meet you. Call me Robert.

Many people believe that *How do you do* is a common response. However, a common response when you are introduced is: *Nice to meet you.*

Note that you only use this the first time you meet someone. If you've met the person before, you say *Nice to see you.* A common response to *Nice to meet you* is *You, too.*

Another common thing to say after meeting someone you have not met before but where it's clear that person introducing you has mentioned this person to you before is:

I've heard a lot about you.

I've heard nice things about you.

I've heard so much about you.

Can you guess what the most common response is to *I've heard a lot about you*? It's *I've heard a lot about you too* or *I hope it was good.*
Another common way to introduce yourself or others is

By the way, I'm Jose.

You will also notice that introductions often happen rather late in a conversation, and sometimes even weeks later.

PRACTICE 1: TITLES

Work with a partner. List some common titles or honorifics used for these people.

Professor or Teacher: _____

Man: _____

Woman: _____

Answer these questions:

1. When do you use a first name only? _____

2. When do you use a last name only? _____

3. When do you use a short first name or a nickname? _____

_____

PRACTICE 2: SITUATIONAL SIMULATIONS

Look at each situation. Decide if you would start a conversation (Y or N) and explain why or why not. Also discuss what topics would be appropriate to talk about.

___ 1. You want to meet with a professor. When you get to his office, another student is waiting to see him, too. You are a freshman and don't know anything about the professor or the department.

   Appropriate topics: _____

   _____

___ 2. You recently declared a major and the department is having a happy hour for newly declared majors to meet other undergraduates, graduate students, TAs, and professors. You attend by yourself. You go up to the table where the food and drinks are. A woman you recognize as the department chairperson's administrative assistant is standing there, too.

   Appropriate topics: _____

   _____

___ 3. You like to play basketball, so you decide to join the university's intramural team, but you don't know anyone else. You arrive at the first organizational meeting and sit down next to someone you don't know a few minutes before the meeting is to begin.

   Appropriate topics: _____

   _____

___ 4. You are locking your bike at a rack outside the building where your class is meeting. Someone else pulls up and begins locking her bike up next to yours.

Appropriate topics: _____

_____

___ 5. Your TA invites all the students to meet for coffee after the session ends. You decide to attend but when you arrive only the TA is there at first.

Appropriate topics: _____

_____

___ 6. You are waiting for the campus shuttle to pick you up to take you back to the dorms/residence halls. You have about five minutes before its scheduled arrival. An older man joins you at the stop.

Appropriate topics: _____

_____

___ 7. You are boarding a plane to Las Vegas for an academic conference. Someone sits down next to you.

Appropriate topics: _____

_____

PRACTICE 3: INTERVIEWS

Find a partner in class that you have not talked to before. Introduce yourselves to each other. Then interview each other. Take notes in the space provided. Find out who they are (name), where they are from, why they are taking this class, and what they like to do. After a few minutes, introduce your partner to the class.

Get Acquainted

Part 1

Complete the tasks in the chart.

Task	Notes (Wording, Responses, Notes about the Interaction)
Introduce yourself to someone you don't know	
Introduce someone you know to someone they don't know	
Describe a situation in which people were not introduced (this can involve you or be something you observed)	

Part 2

Choose someplace you visit regularly or are interested in learning more about. Observe the location for one hour. Take notes on how people greet, introduce themselves and others, and say goodbye. Write a report with five observations about the wording, the responses, and the factors that may or may not affect the interaction.

Example:

Location: Campus Coffeehouse

I noticed that every time a customer reaches the register, the cashier greets them, introduces himself, and then asks for their order in a friendly tone and with rising intonation. Hi, my name is Jake. What can I get for you?

PRACTICE 4: ANALYSIS

Work with a group. Compare your Get Acquainted charts and answer these questions.

1. Are introductions required? Could you have the same or similar experiences without having formal introductions?

2. In many cases, English is formulaic. You can predict what a person will say and prepare some phrases that are easy for you to remember and pronounce. Do you see any patterns to the introductions and responses?

3. What notes do you have about each interaction? Did these affect the interactions? Did this affect the patterns you noticed?

Unit 2

Giving Opinions, Agreeing, and Disagreeing

Part 1: Giving Opinions

Discussion Starter

- How often do you give your opinion? Are there any times when you do not give your opinion? When? What might affect your decision about giving your opinion?

- When you are in your home country, which topics is it okay to give your opinions on? Which topics are not okay to discuss openly?

- Are there any individuals to whom you may not want to tell your opinion? Why?

Language Lesson: Expressing Likes and Dislikes

There are degrees of how much you might like or dislike something.

I like . . .	I don't like . . .
I love . . .	I dislike . . .
I enjoy . . .	I don't care for . . .
I'm happy about . . .	I hate . . .
I'm thrilled with . . .	. . . bother/annoys me . . .
That's a great . . .	I can't stand . . .

PRACTICE 1: EXPRESSING LIKES AND DISLIKES

Answer these questions with a partner or small group.

1. How would you rank the like and dislike phrases in order of strength? List them from strongest to weakest.

2. What other phrases or words would you add to the lists?

3. Which do you think are most common?

Language Lesson: Expressing Opinions

Expressing your opinion in English-speaking settings is common. Speakers need to express their opinions in social, academic, and professional contexts and with a variety of speakers—peers, bosses, friends, and strangers. Native speakers preface their opinions using a variety of words and phrases.

Some of these opinion language phrases are more common than others. *I think* is the most common.

I think/I believe/I feel . . .	It seems to me that . . .
The point I'm making is . . .	As I see it . . .
In my opinion . . .	If you ask me . . .
To me . . .	My feeling is . . . / I feel like . . .

I think having a second language is a valuable skill.

Pronunciation Note: Native speakers may use a hesitation device or filler before using one of the phrases to ease their way in or to soften (not sound too forward) such as

So [pause] . . .

Well [pause] . . .

Umm [pause] . . .

Hmm [pause] . . .

Well [pause], I think having a second language is a valuable skill.

PRACTICE 2: GIVING YOUR OPINION

Work with a partner. Take turns giving your opinions about some of the topics listed. Use opinion language or like/dislike language.

1. campus safety

2. homework

3. organic food

4. electric cars

5. college entrance exams (TOEFL®, GRE®, SAT)

6. your most recent vacation destination

PRACTICE 3: COMMONALITY

Some phrases are used more frequently than others. Divide the phrases from the Language Lesson on Expressing Opinions into two categories based on what you have observed.

1. Categorize the opinion phrases into which you think are more common and which are less common.

More Common	Less Common

2. Search the Corpus of Contemporary American English (COCA) to see how frequently each of the phrases appears.

a. Go to http://corpus.byu.edu/coca/.

b. In the box, enter each phrase listed.

c. Write the quantity of appearances for each phrase.

I think: _____

I believe: _____

I feel like: _____

The point I'm making is: _____

In my opinion: _____

To me: _____

My feeling is: _____

It seems to me that: _____

As I see it: _____

If you ask me: _____

3. Discuss these questions with a partner.

a. What surprised you?

b. Which of these phrases have you heard used? What was the context?

c. Which of these phrases do you want to use more often based on the results? Less often?

Language Lesson: What to Say When You Are Less Than Certain

What should you do if you want to express your opinion, but you are not 100 percent sure about your answer? For example, what do you say when a teacher asks you a question in class or someone poses a question during a class discussion but you are not sure of the answer?

It is understandable that someone may not want to say anything when they are not sure, but sometimes this is not an option. There is language that can help you in these cases. You should try to answer, but you can preface your opinion (words and phrases from the first language lesson in this unit) with phrasing to let the other participants know that you are not claiming to know something perfectly. Your tone can also convey that you're not trying to say you are absolutely certain about what you are going to say.

I'm not sure, but . . .	I have some doubts, but . . .
I don't know, but . . .	I'm not 100 percent sure, but . . .
I don't know, but I'm starting to think that . . .	I won't swear to this, but . . .

These can also be preceded by hesitation devices or fillers.

Do you think democracy is the best form of government?

Well, I don't know, but I think it is because all citizens who are eligible get to participate equally.

Maybe, but I think it is because all citizens who are eligible get to participate equally.

PRACTICE 1: GIVING LESS-THAN-CERTAIN OPINIONS

Work with a partner. Pick at least three topics from the list about which you are not 100 percent sure. Take turns giving your opinions.

1. salaries of professors

2. self-driving cars

3. the university plagiarism policy

4. U.S. political elections

5. taxes on soft drinks

6. solar energy

PRACTICE 2: ASKING FOR OPINIONS

Asking for an opinion can keep a conversation going. Plus, it shows the other participants that you are interested in hearing what they have to say.

Work with a partner. Use a sentence frame from Column 1 and a topic from Column 2 to ask each other for opinions. Use the language from this unit's Language Lessons to express likes or dislikes or to give opinions. Write the opinions in Column 3. Be careful! Not all frames work with all topics. For example, a native speaker is not likely to say, "Are you in favor of modern art?"

Column 1: Sentence Frames	Column 2: Topics	Column 3: Opinions
What do you think about . . .	Hazing	
How do you feel about . . .	Death penalty	
Are you opposed to . . .	Internships	
Are you for (in favor of) . . .	Legalized marijuana	
What are your thoughts on . . .	College admissions requirements	
What's your opinion on . . .	Modern art	
Tell me what you believe/think / feel about . . .	Violence in video games (or in movies)	

Part 2: Agreeing and Disagreeing

- Which is easier: agreeing or disagreeing? Support your answer.

- Which fuels discussion: agreeing or disagreeing? Support your answer.

- How does agreeing affect an interaction? How does disagreeing affect an interaction?

Language Lesson: Agreeing and Disagreeing

Use **agreeing** words and phrases to let someone know you have the same opinion.

What You Learned	What Is More Common
I agree./I agree with you.	Absolutely.
I feel the same way.	You can say that again.
I couldn't agree more.	I hear you.
That's exactly what I think.	For sure.
That's my opinion, too.	Right. / You're right.
	Yep.
	That's [so] true.
	Me, too.
	Exactly.
	I think so, too.

Don't be afraid to **disagree**. Disagreement keeps conversations alive.

What You Learned	*What Is More Common*
I disagree./I disagree with you. I disagree with what you're saying. I don't agree./I don't agree with you.	I don't think so. I don't see it that way.

Pronunciation Note: There are some very informal ways to disagree. These would obviously be reserved for informal situations or for people you know very well. These are usually in yes/no question format and use rising intonation. How can a person's tone make the disagreement better or worse?

Are you kidding?   Are you serious?

Are you crazy?   You're not serious?

Did you want to make me laugh?   You don't believe that, do you?

You know that's crazy, right?

Sometimes native speakers talk with another person about someone else that they have agreed with.

Did you hear what Patricia said in class?

Yeah. I totally disagree with her. I think there are times that the death penalty is not the best solution.

You might agree with part of what someone says. In those cases, you can partially agree, which lets the other participants that know you disagree with only part of what was said.

What You Learned	What Is More Common (Especially in Less Formal Situations):
I respect your opinion, but . . .	I don't think so.
You have a right to your opinion, but . . .	I see what you're saying . . .
I understand what you're saying, but . . .	True, but . . .
That's true, but . . .	No.
You could be right, but . . .	Are you sure? / You sure?
I see your point, but . . .	Not me.
I hate to disagree with you, but . . .	I'm not so sure.
I don't completely agree . . .	But don't you think . . .
You have to remember that . . .	Yes, but . . .
	Okay, but . . .
	Right, but . . .
	I agree, but . . .
	But what if . . .
	Are you forgetting that . . .
	Get outta here!
	No way!

PRACTICE 1: SITUATIONAL ANALYSIS

Work with a partner or small group. For each situation, decide if you would (Y) or would not (N) express your opinion and if you would use a more formal phrase (F) or informal phrase (I) during the conversation. Be prepared to explain your choices. An example has been done for you.

1. Talking with a friend about a movie that he/she really liked but you thought was terrible. __Y__   __I__

2. You are talking with a friend you have known for many years who is having a baby and just told you the baby's name. You do not like the name. _____   _____

3. A group of classmates are talking about the drinking age in the United States. _____   _____

4. You are meeting with colleagues at the office about the election results. Your colleagues like the new president, but you don't like him/her. _____   _____

5. You're on a date and your date asks what kind of food you want to eat. _____   _____

6. You're talking to your roommate about the new quiet hours at the dorm. _____   _____

7. Your advisor calls you in to ask about your grades in other classes. _____   _____

8. You see your professor at the bookstore and start talking about the book he/she is buying. _____   _____

PRACTICE 2: AGREEING AND DISAGREEING ABOUT PROFESSIONAL IDEAS

Read the document provided by the U.S. Department of Agriculture. Choose three statements and talk with a partner about why you agree or disagree with them.

Top 10 Things You Need to Know About the 2015–2020 Dietary Guidelines for Americans

Posted on January 7, 2016, by ODPHP

The Dietary Guidelines provides a clear path to help Americans eat healthfully, informed by a critical and transparent review of the scientific evidence on nutrition.

1. A lifetime of healthy eating helps to prevent chronic diseases like obesity, heart disease, high blood pressure, and Type 2 diabetes.

2. Healthy eating is one of the most powerful tools we have to reduce the onset of disease. The Dietary Guidelines recommendations can help you make informed choices about eating for you and your family.

3. The path to improving health through nutrition is to follow a healthy eating pattern that's right for you. Eating patterns are the combination of foods and drinks you eat over time. A healthy eating pattern is adaptable to a person's taste preferences, traditions, culture, and budget.

4. A healthy eating pattern includes:

   - A variety of vegetables: dark green, red and orange, legumes (beans and peas), starchy, and other vegetables

   - Fruits, especially whole fruit

   - Grains, at least half of which are whole grain

- Fat-free or low-fat dairy, including milk, yogurt, cheese, and/or fortified soy beverages

- A variety of protein foods, including seafood, lean meats and poultry, eggs, legumes (beans and peas), soy products, and nuts and seeds

- Oils, including those from plants: canola, corn, olive, peanut, safflower, soybean, and sunflower. Oils also are naturally present in nuts, seeds, seafood, olives, and avocados.

5. Healthy eating patterns limit added sugars. Less than 10% of your daily calories should come from added sugars. ChooseMyPlate.gov provides more information about added sugars, which are sugars and syrups that are added to foods or beverages when they are processed or prepared. This does not include naturally occurring sugars such as those consumed as part of milk and fruits.

6. Healthy eating patterns limit saturated and trans fats. Less than 10% of your daily calories should come from saturated fats. Foods that are high in saturated fat include butter, whole milk, meats that are not labeled as lean, and tropical oils such as coconut and palm oil. Saturated fats should be replaced with unsaturated fats, such as canola or olive oil.

7. Healthy eating patterns limit sodium. Adults and children ages 14 years and over should limit sodium to less than 2,300 mg per day, and children younger than 14 years should consume even less. Use the Nutrition Facts label to check for sodium, especially in processed foods like pizza, pasta dishes, sauces, and soups.

8. Most Americans can benefit from making small shifts in their daily eating habits to improve their health over the long run. Small shifts in food choices—over the course of a week, a day, or even a meal—can make a difference in working toward a healthy eating pattern that works for you.

9. Remember physical activity! Regular physical activity is one of the most important things individuals can do to improve their health. According to the Department of Health and Human Services' Physical Activity Guidelines for Americans, adults need at least 150 minutes of moderate intensity physical activity each week and should perform muscle-strengthening exercises on two or more days each week. Children ages 6 to 17 years need at least 60 minutes of physical activity per day, including aerobic, muscle-strengthening, and bone-strengthening activities.

10. Everyone has a role—at home, schools, workplaces, communities, and food retail outlets—in encouraging easy, accessible, and affordable ways to support healthy choices.

- At **home, you and your family** can try out small changes to find what works for you like adding more veggies to favorite dishes, planning meals and cooking at home, and incorporating physical activity into time with family or friends.

- **Schools** can improve the selection of healthy food choices in cafeterias and vending machines, provide nutrition education programs and school gardens, increase school-based physical activity, and encourage parents and caregivers to promote healthy changes at home.

- **Workplaces** can encourage walking or activity breaks; offer healthy food options in the cafeteria, vending machines, and at staff meetings or functions; and provide health and wellness programs and nutrition counseling.

- **Communities** can increase access to affordable, healthy food choices through community gardens, farmers' markets, shelters, and food banks and create walkable communities by maintaining safe public spaces.

- **Food retail outlets** can inform consumers about making healthy changes and provide healthy food choices.

From: https://health.gov/news/dietary-guidelines-digital-press-kit/2016/01/top-10-things-you-need-to-know/

PRACTICE 3: GROUP DISCUSSION

Imagine your group has been hired by the university to develop a handbook for new international students. Discuss the questions and use the language from this unit. Use the opinion, agreeing (fully or partially), and disagreeing phrases. Do not be afraid to disagree until you come to a consensus. Be prepared to present the information that will go in your handbook to the other groups. Think about your tone when agreeing and disagreeing during the discussion. A few examples are given.

1. Where is the best place to eat on campus?

   I think the best place is Pizza House.

   I disagree. It's Steve's Diner.

2. When is the best time to go to the library?

   I'm not sure, but I think the best time to go to the library is 6 PM when everyone else is at dinner.

3. Where do you recommend parents stay when they visit?

4. What should tourists or new students see on campus?

5. Who are the best teachers to take classes from?

6. What are the best classes to take your first year?

7. Where can you find the best tutoring help?

8. What times are the most popular for classes?

9. What is the best way to make American friends?

10. Why do you recommend other international students choose this school?

PRACTICE 4: PROFESSIONAL GROUP DISCUSSION

Part 1

Opinions, agreeing, and disagreeing language is something you will not only use socially but also professionally. Being able to support your opinions with reasons or facts can fuel a discussion.

Write pros and cons for this topic:

International students should spend at least one summer interning at a U.S. company before they graduate.

Pros: _____

_____

_____

_____

Cons: _____

_____

_____

_____

Share your ideas with a small group.

Part 2

Choose one of these topics, fill in the blanks, circle one of the options in bold, and talk about your opinions. Once you all agree on the general statement, compile a list of pros and cons with your group. Be prepared to share your list with the other groups.

_____ are paid **too much/not enough** for the work they do.

_____ **is/is not** a good social networking platform.

_____ **is/is not** a good television show.

Taxes on _____ **should/should not** be higher.

Working mothers **do/do not** _____.

Governments **should/should not** pay for _____.

Pros: _____

_____

_____

_____

Cons: _____

_____

_____

_____

Get Acquainted

Ask two people the two questions. Write their answers, and make sure to notice the opinion language they use. For an extra challenge, adapt the questions using a variety of opinion sentence frames to ask the questions.

Question	Answers/Notes	

Who do you think is the best U.S. President?
  a. Abraham Lincoln
  b. John F. Kennedy
  c. Ronald Reagan
  d. Barack Obama
Why?
	Person 1 Answer	Person 1 Opinion Language

	Person 2 Answer	Person 2 Opinion Language
What do you think is the most important political issue in the United States right now?	Person 1 Answer	
	Person 2 Answer	

PRACTICE 5: ANALYSIS

Work with a group. Compare your Get Acquainted charts and answer these questions.

1. Were people firm in their opinions or did some people use language expressing some uncertainty?

2. In many cases, English is formulaic. You can predict what a person will say and prepare some phrases that are easy for you to remember and pronounce. What are some common phrases that your group noticed?

3. Is this a sensitive topic in your own country? How did people respond here when you asked?

4. What notes do you recall about each interaction? Did these affect the interactions?

5. Did you hear any words/phrases that you had not heard before? Did you know what they meant?

Unit 3

Using the Phone

Discussion Starter

- How often do you use the phone? Do you like or dislike it?

- What kinds of calls do you make?

- What do you find challenging about talking on the phone in English? How does this list change if you are using your native language?

- How has technology—such as mobile phones or Skype and Facetime—changed the way we communicate via phone—in terms of quality or quantity?

Language Lesson: Phone Calls

A phone call generally begins with three parts after the person answering says *Hello*.

- o greeting

- o identification

- o purpose of call

As with other patterns of communication, this is probably less formal than what you learned before.

What You Learned	*What Is More Common*
Hello. My name is Yuping. May I speak to Connie, please?	Hello, This is Yuping. Is Connie home? Hello, Is Connie there? Hello, Is Connie available? Hello, Is Connie busy?

Notice that:

- the greeting may sometimes be less formal than you would expect.

- the identification may be more specific or more general depending on who you are calling, who answers the phone, and the purpose. Sometimes, it may not even be used.

- the purpose can take many forms.

Examples:

Hi. Is Kathy home/there?

Hello. I'm a new customer and I'm having trouble with my phone bill.

Hello. I'm a patient. I need to make an appointment with Dr. Bunting.

Hi. I'm a friend of Rick's. Is he there?

Hello. Is Professor Lockwood there?

Hello. Can I talk to/be transferred to the manager?

Pronunciation Note: Enunciation is speaking clearly in order to be understood. It is different than pronunciation in that pronunciation often focuses on the making sounds correctly, such as word stress, clustering groups of letters, or saying individual sounds the right way. In other words, you may pronounce a word correctly, but if you are too quiet or mumble the word, then you are not enunciating and the listener cannot hear you. It is very important in phone or online communications that you enunciate so that the loss of non-verbal cues (phone) or technical interference (Skype, Facetime, and the like) do not affect the interaction.

PRACTICE 1: PATTERNS

Many phone interactions fall into patterns. Work with a partner. Read the scripts from actual phone calls and then complete the script. Make sure to consider who the speakers are.

1. Friends

   Caller: Hey, it's me.

   Answerer: _____

2. Doctor's Office

   Answerer: Dr. Mizuki's Office.

   Caller: _____

3. Phone Interview

   Caller: My name is Joe from HR at Google. Is this Yiheng?

   Answerer: _____

   Caller: Is this still a good time to talk?

   Answerer: _____

4. Wrong Number

Answerer: Hello.

Caller: Can I talk to [someone who doesn't live / work there]?

Answerer: _____

Caller: _____

5. Answering for Someone Else

Answerer: Hello.

Caller: Hello. Is Fernando there?

Answerer [to Caller]: _____

Answerer [to Fernando]: _____

6. Answering for Someone Else Who Isn't Home/Available

Answerer: Hello.

Caller: Hello. Is Fernando there?

Answerer: _____

PRACTICE 2: WHAT DO YOU SAY WHEN?

Work with a partner. Talk about each situation and decide what to say.

What do you say when:

1. calling your professor at home and his/her spouse answers the phone?

   _____

2. calling your friend Mikhail at his summer internship company and an administrative assistant answers the phone?

   _____

3. calling a classmate you don't know well and someone else answers the phone?

   _____

4. calling Verizon about a mistake on your phone bill?

   _____

5. calling a good friend and her mother answers the phone?

   _____

6. calling a company to make sure they have received your resume?

   _____

7. calling the Registrar to request a copy of your transcript be sent to a graduate program.

   _____

8. calling a professor to request a meeting to talk about which classes to take next term.

   _____

PRACTICE 3: VOICE MAIL

Write an answer for each of the messages. <u>Note:</u> A good rule of thumb is to leave only the information requested and to keep the message brief. If your instructor asks, highlight or underline stressed syllables and words and/or write how it will sound in English (not how it is supposed to sound). See the Appendix for more information.

What do you say when:

1. the message says, "I can't take your call right now, but leave your name, number, and message and I'll call you back as soon as I can."

   _____

2. the message says, "Your call is important to Mayne Gas and Electric Utility Company. Please leave your name and number and someone from customer service will return your call within two business days.

   _____

3. the message says, "I'm out of my office right now, but leave your name, the time you called, and a short message and I'll call you back.

   _____

4. the message says, "Dr. Venturi's office is now closed. Leave your contact information and a good time to call you back and someone from his staff will call you back tomorrow. If this is an emergency, please call Dr. Venturi's emergency line.

   _____

5. the message says, "No one can take your call right now. Leave a message!"

   _____

PRACTICE 4: INFORMATION

Find these numbers.

1. Emergency for off-campus help: _____

2. Emergency for on-campus help (campus security): _____

3. Local time and temperature number: _____

4. International code for the United States: _____

5. International code to call your country from the United States:

   _____

6. Way to dial extensions on campus: _____

7. IT support/help on campus: _____

8. Information: _____

9. Who to call to get cable, electricity, or water turned on:

   _____

10. How to get on the No Call List: _____

Language Lesson: Giving Numerical Information

To say an address or room number with one digit, say the number as a whole number: 6 Main Street [six]

To say an address or room number with two digits, say the whole number (not two individual numbers): 25 Main Street [twenty-five, NOT two five]

To say an address or room number with three digits, say the first number as a single digit and say the last two as a whole number: 522 Main Street [five twenty-two]

To say an address or room number with four digits, say them as two whole numbers with a small pause between them: 6298 Main Street [sixty-two, pause, ninety-eight]

To say the area code of a phone number and/or the first three digits of a phone number, say them as single whole numbers: 212-555-8265 [two one two]

To say the last four numbers of a phone number, say the first two as single digits, make a slight pause, and then say the last two as single digits: 212-555-8265 [two one two, pause, five five five, pause, eight two, slight pause, six five]

Option: For the last four digits, you can say them as two whole numbers with a slight pause in between: 212-555-8265 [two one two, pause, five five five, pause, eighty-two, slight pause, sixty-five]

Note: Do not "mix and match." In other words, do not say the first two as single digits and the last two as a whole number.

If the address, room numbers, or phone number is a multiple of 1000 (like many company numbers), say it that way: 2000 Main Street [two thousand] or 212-555-4000 [two one two, pause, five five five, pause, four thousand]

PRACTICE 5: SCRIPTS

1. Practice saying your U.S. phone number. Pronounce the numbers with proper pausing and groupings.

2. Practice spelling your name. Pronounce each letter correctly. Think of a way to help someone understand your name. For example *My name is Yuan. It is spelled Y-U-A-N. It sounds like UN, like the United Nations.* Or, *My name is Yuan. That's spelled Y as in "yellow," U as in. . . .*

3. Practice giving your address with the proper numbers and spelling of the street names.

4. Often you can use the same voicemail message in a variety of situations. Write a script that you can use that is easy to pronounce. Include your name and phone number. Include other details you think you might need, such as when you will be available for them to call you back. As noted in Practice 3, keep it brief. Then practice the script with a partner. Make sure to read the script with the right rhythm and pronunciation.

_____

_____

_____

PRACTICE 6: MAKING IMPROVEMENTS

Improve the final part of each dialogue.

1. Answerer: Hello.

   Caller: Is Lea there?

   Answerer: ~~Who is this?~~ _____

2. Answerer: Hello.

   Caller: Is Lea there?

   Answerer: ~~No. What do you want?~~ _____

3. Answerer: Hello.

   Caller: Is Lea there?

   Answerer: ~~Wrong number.~~ _____

4. Answerer: University Bookstore.

   Caller: ~~I want to talk to a manager.~~ _____

5. Answerer: Hello.

   Caller. ~~I am Marco.~~ _____

6. Answerer: Dr. Jensen's Office.

    Caller: ~~I need the doctor.~~ _____

7. Answerer: Hello.

    Caller: Is Jen home?

    Answerer: She's not here right now.

    Caller: ~~Tell her to call me.~~ _____

PRACTICE 7: ROLE-PLAYS

Work with a partner to write a role-play for each situation. If your instructor asks, highlight or underline stressed syllables and words and/or write how it will sound in English (not how it is supposed to sound). (See the Appendix.)

1. You are friends. You need to call to borrow the notes from class. Make arrangements to get the notes and find out when to return them.

2. You are a student and advisor. The student wants to talk about courses to take next term. Have a short conversation and make an appointment to talk in more detail.

3. You are a student calling a program that offers conversation partners. The program administrative assistant answers the phone. Explain that you are calling for a friend who doesn't know much English. Find out more details about the program (times, dates, costs).

4. You answer the phone and it is someone who wants you to take a survey about political issues.

5. Your car broke down. You call for roadside assistance.

PRACTICE 8: TEXTING

More and more people are communicating via text. Answer these questions with a partner.

1. In what situations is it better to text than to call? In what situations should you not text?

2. Who should you text or not text?

3. When should you text or not text?

4. How long should text messages be? Why might you want to limit the length or amount of texts you send someone?

5. How long should it take a person to respond to your text? What might affect the response time?

6. What grammar and spelling rules should be followed? Can they change?

7. Write an appropriate text message for each situation:

   a. borrowing notes from a friend: _____

   b. meeting your roommate for lunch: _____

   c. being late to a meeting: _____

   d. looking for a classmate who is not in class: _____

   e. asking someone to meet for coffee: _____

8. Write a text message you use often. Share it with the class.

   _____

PRACTICE 9: GROUP ACTIVITY: PHONE ETIQUETTE

Make a list of the five most important rules to follow when talking on the phone. You can include three from the list, but add two of your own.

- Don't take personal calls when you are working.

- Don't do other things (for example, check email or social media) when you are on the phone.

- Use an appropriate tone of voice based on who you are talking to and what you are talking about.

- Don't take another call when you are talking to someone.

- Don't interrupt speakers.

- Don't make calls while in public places (in restaurants, on trains/public transportation).

- Don't make calls outside in noisy settings, such as near traffic or construction.

- Enunciate.

- Let the call go to voicemail when. . . .

- Tell people when you are using a mobile phone or web service in case the call drops or you experience technical difficulty. You may also want to provide your phone number for them to all you back if the call drops.

Get Acquainted

Part 1

Get this information from a phone call.

Information Needed	Information Found	Phone Number/Location Called
How much does a transcript cost?		
How late is the library you use most often open?		
What is being served today at your favorite campus eatery?		
How soon could you get an appointment at the writing center?		

Part 2

Write a short report about a phone call you need to make. For example, describe making a reservation at a restaurant, calling your professor, calling a company to get information or help, calling to set up a job interview, or any other type of call. Complete this report.

Who did you call?

What was the purpose of your call?

What language did you notice (yours and the answerer)?

What patterns did you notice?

What was the result of the interaction?

PRACTICE 10: ANALYSIS

Work with a group. Compare your Get Acquainted charts/reports and answer these questions.

1. What made this call easy or challenging?

2. How would this have changed if you had tried doing this online (using the internet) or face-to-face?

3. In many cases, English is formulaic. You can predict what a person will say and prepare some phrases that are easy for you to remember and pronounce. Did the call follow any patterns presented in this unit?

4. What was your tone of voice? What about the person you talked to? Can the tone of voice change the interaction?

Unit 4

Offering and Asking
for Assistance

Part 1: Offering Assistance

Discussion Starter

- What kinds of things do you ask for help with?

- Has anyone ever turned you down when you asked for assistance? When you've offered assistance?

- Make a list of people you are comfortable asking for assistance from. Then make a list of people to whom you offer assistance.

Language Lesson: Offering Assistance

How do you offer to help someone?

Some of these offers might be more familiar to you than others.

How may/can I help you?	Do you need/want some help?
May/Can I help you?	What can I do for you?
Can I help out?	What do you need?
How can I be of service/help you?	Want me to help you?
	Want/Need a hand?
Would you like some help/assistance?	Are you having trouble/Do you have a problem?

Notice the use of modals. **Modals** are often used to make the questions more polite or formal. However, some offers are more direct. These phrases are used especially when the situation seems urgent (as in when someone seems like they need help immediately). For example, what would you say when someone is carrying a heavy box and it looks like they are about to drop it. Remember that tone of voice is important here as well. What do you think you should say? How should you say it?

Also beware of tone. If you say the word *problem* the "wrong" way in *Do you have a problem?* it can sound like you are angry or that you do not like the person.

Direct Offers

Wait. Let me help you.

Let me help out.

Here. Let me get that for you.

Let me give you a hand.

I'll get that [for you].

Pronunciation Note: The offers of assistance that are in the form of a yes/no question are asked with rising intonation. The direct offers are statements and sometimes immediately followed by the help whether the other person accepts that offer or not.

PRACTICE 1: FORMALITY

For each phrase, list a location where you think you are likely to hear each phrase. Then write the phrase with the pronunciation you are most likely to hear.

Phrase	Location	Pronunciation
May I help you?		
Let me give you a hand.		
Would you like some help?		
What can I do for you?		
I'll get that for you.		
How can I be of service?		

Based on your answers in the chart, discuss these questions with a partner.

1. When is it better to use more formal language when offering assistance?

2. Who do you feel comfortable using the more direct language with?

3. How do factors such as age, gender, relationship, or status make a difference when offering assistance?

Language Lesson: Responses and Second Offers

Responses can be positive (accept your offer) or negative (reject your offer). Note that it isn't always "bad" if your offer is turned down.

Do you need some help?

Accept	Reject
Thanks.	No thanks. / Thanks anyway.
Yeah, that'd be great.	No, that's okay. I got it.
Sure, please.	I'm all right.
I'd appreciate that.	It's okay. I can manage.

Second Offers

Sometimes when people say no, the asker will ask again. The response may or may not change.

"I'm all right."

You sure?

Really, I don't mind.

Seriously. I'm heading that way anyway.

PRACTICE 2: RESPONSES

Read each situation. Write a possible offer, response to accept, and response to reject the offer. Be prepared to explain your choices.

1. Your English teacher is carrying a heavy bag to the classroom.

   Your Offer: _____

   Acceptance: _____

   Rejection: _____

   Rationale: _____

   _____

2. Your see a classmate at the library studying for an engineering midterm you both have the next day. This is an easy class for you, but your classmate has mentioned that this is a hard class for him.

   Your Offer: _____

   Acceptance: _____

   Rejection: _____

   Rationale: _____

   _____

3. Your neighbors are going on vacation. You offer to pick up their newspaper and mail while they are away.

   Your Offer: _____

   Acceptance: _____

   Rejection: _____

   Rationale: _____

   _____

4. Your advisor invites you to dinner at her house. You offer to help clear the table.

   Your Offer: _____

   Acceptance: _____

   Rejection: _____

   Rationale: _____

   _____

5. A friend has a flat tire on his bike and is trying to fix it. You offer to help even though you don't know much about bike repair.

   Your Offer: _____

   Acceptance: _____

   Rejection: _____

   Rationale: _____

   _____

6. Your roommate can't find his chemistry textbook. You have no idea where it is and you really need to leave for another class.

Your Offer: _____

Acceptance: _____

Rejection: _____

Rationale: _____

_____

7. You see an older person having trouble opening the doors at the shopping mall.

Your Offer: _____

Acceptance: _____

Rejection: _____

Rationale: _____

_____

8. You're walking on campus and see someone looking at a map on their phone.

Your Offer: _____

Acceptance: _____

Rejection: _____

Rationale: _____

_____

Get Acquainted

Interview someone who is from the United States. Ask these questions and take notes on their responses.

Question	Notes
How would you offer assistance if you worked at a hotel?	
How would you offer assistance if a friend needed help with homework?	
Would you offer to help a stranger who had car trouble?	
What would you suggest someone do if you aren't able to help someone?	
What reasons might you give someone when you can't help them?	

PRACTICE 3: ANALYSIS

Work with a group. Compare your Get Acquainted charts and answer these questions.

1. What factors affect the formality of an offer to help?

2. In many cases, English is formulaic. You can predict what a person will say and prepare some phrases that are easy for you to remember and pronounce. What are some common reasons people have for not being able to help?

3. What can you do when you want to help someone but are unable to?

Part 2: Asking for Assistance

Discussion Starter

- What are some circumstances for which you might need to ask for assistance?

- What makes it easy to ask for assistance? What makes it harder?

- Do these circumstances change the way you ask for help?

  o asking for money

  o borrowing a computer

  o needing help when your car breaks down

  o asking for help with homework

Language Lesson: Asking for Assistance

There are some very formal ways to ask for assistance. Notice that these phrases are longer (use more words) and use modals (to add a degree of politeness).

If it's not too much trouble, could/would you . . .	Could I impose on you for a minute?
	Would you be willing to . . .
I hope you don't mind, but could/would you . . .	I hate to ask, but . . .
Would you mind . . .	I'm sorry to bother you, but . . .
Can I ask a favor? Could/Would you . . .	I was wondering if you could/would . . .

Like offering assistance, requests for assistance can be more direct. These are usually shorter and may not use modals.

Can you help me?   Lend me a dollar?

Can you give me a hand?   Do you have a minute to help me?

How about helping me with . . .   Can you give me [a ride home]?

Do you think you could . . .   Mind if I [use your pen for a sec]?

These phrases might be preceded by *Excuse me*.

Direct requests may not always be in the form of a question.

I need some help.

Get the [book] for me, [will you]?

Lend me your study notes for a minute.

Let me see your notes for a minute.

People can accept (give you help) or reject (not give you help). If they reject, they usually offer a reason for their rejection and may offer a possible alternate.

Can you give me a ride home?

Accept: Sure, it's on my way.

Reject: I'm sorry, I can't. I didn't drive. But, we can ask my friend for a ride.

Can you help me study?

Accept: Sure.

Reject: *I want to, but I have to leave for class. How about later?*

PRACTICE 1: HOW DO YOU ASK?

Work with a partner. Choose an appropriate phrase in terms of formality
and directness for each situation.

How do you ask . . .

1. a professor or teacher for help with a research paper?

   _____

2. a stranger for directions?

   _____

3. a neighbor if you can borrow a can opener?

   _____

4. a friend to help you proofread your resume?

   _____

5. a classmate you don't know if you can borrow a pen?

   _____

6. a good friend to pick you up after work?

   _____

7. a librarian how to find a journal article?

   _____

8. an employee at the phone store how to fix your phone?

_____

9. a customer service agent at the credit card company about a problem with your bill?

_____

PRACTICE 2: RESPONSES

Write an acceptance and rejection for each of the situations in Practice 1.

1. a professor or teacher for help with a research paper

   Accept: _____

   Reject: _____

2. a stranger for directions

   Accept: _____

   Reject: _____

3. a neighbor if you can borrow a can opener

   Accept: _____

   Reject: _____

4. a friend to help you proofread your resume

   Accept: _____

   Reject: _____

5. a classmate you don't know if you can borrow a pen

Accept: _____

Reject: _____

6. a good friend to pick you up after work

Accept: _____

Reject: _____

7. a librarian how to find a journal article

Accept: _____

Reject: _____

8. an employee at the phone store how to fix your phone

Accept: _____

Reject: _____

9. a customer service agent at the credit card company about a problem with your bill

Accept: _____

Reject: _____

PRACTICE 3: ROLE-PLAYS

Work with a partner. Write a role-play for one of these situations.

1. You just arrived on campus and want to open an American bank account. You walk into the bank . . .

2. You want to buy a car. You want to ask a friend to go with you since you've never bought a car before.

3. You want your English teacher to proofread a cover letter for an internship you want to apply for. This is not part of his or her job.

4. You are on vacation and you want to ask a stranger to take your picture in front of a famous landmark.

Get Acquainted

You are going on an English scavenger hunt. Ask people who were born in the United States to help you with your homework. Complete the chart.

Task	Their Answer	Language You Used to Ask for Assistance	Language They Used to Accept / Reject	Notes about the Interaction (Gender, Age, Location, Time, etc.)
Meaning of *head and shoulders above the rest*				
Definition of *bewilder*				
Example of a simile or metaphor				
Recommended American novel to read				
Sentence using the idiom *wet blanket*				

PRACTICE 4: ANALYSIS

Work with a group. Compare your Get Acquainted charts and answer these questions.

1. When were you more formal? Why?

2. Were people willing to help you? Why do you think this happened? Does the language you choose make a difference in people's willingness to help?

3. What hindered the exchange? Would you do anything differently?

4. What notes do you have about each interaction? Did these affect the interactions?

Unit 5

Asking for and Giving Advice

Part 1: Asking for Advice

Discussion Starter

- What kinds of advice did your parents give you when you were growing up?

- What advice would you offer someone who is thinking of going into your field?

- If you were having trouble with your classes, who would you ask for advice from? Why?

Language Lesson: Asking for Advice

There are many reasons to ask for advice. What are some things for which you have asked for advice?

There are certain words and phrases generally used to ask for advice.

How do I . . .	What do you recommend/suggest?
What would you do?	Any advice on . . .
Do you think I should . . .	Any ideas? / Any ideas on . . .
What do you think would help?	If this was you . . .
What should I do?	

<u>Note:</u> The correct grammar is *If this were you*, but native speakers do not always use correct grammar.

> If you were me, what would you do?

> What do you think I should do?

Pronunciation Note: Native English speakers often link their words. **Linking** is connecting words to each other. The words will not sound the same as when they are spoken separately. Although linking is not clearly enunciated, it is very common. Recognizing linking will help you understand people more easily and help others understand you because you will sound more natural.

There are two main types of linking:

o Consonant to vowel: Words that end with a consonant sound link to words beginning with a vowel sound.

o Vowel to vowel: Words ending with a vowel sound link to words beginning with a vowel sound.

Examples:

How do I sounds like *How dooeye* (the *do* and *I* sound like one word).

What do you think sounds like *Whaddayathink*?

Should I sounds like Shouldeye.

PRACTICE 1: PARTICIPANTS

Decide which phrase you would use to ask for advice from each person.

1. student to professor: Wants to get better grade on paper

   _____

2. friend to friend: Wants to know the best teacher in the [English] department

   _____

3. student to professor: Wants to learn English faster

   _____

4. intern to boss: Hopes to advance with the company

   _____

5. classmate to classmate: Needs to know best place to take visitors for dinner

   _____

6. patient to doctor: Wants to know how to treat a cold

   _____

PRACTICE 2: DISCUSSION

Answer these questions with a partner.

1. Do you think any of these situations are easier than others when seeking advice? Which were easiest? Why?

2. Why did you choose the phrases you chose for each situation? How do factors such as age, gender, relationship, or status make a difference when asking for advice? Does tone of voice make a difference?

3. How do linking words and phrases sound as opposed to when they are not linked?

4. What advice would you offer for each of the situations in Practice 1?

Get Acquainted

Interview an American friend or classmate and ask for their advice. Take notes on the language they use and their answers.

Question	Notes
Where do you recommend I take my parents for dinner when they visit?	
Any advice on what kind of car to buy?	
What do you think would help if I had a cold?	
Which classes do you suggest that first-year students take?	
If you were me and had to choose between [Major] and [Major], which would you choose?	

PRACTICE 3: ANALYSIS

Work with a group. Compare your Get Acquainted charts and answer these questions.

1. In many cases, English is formulaic. You can predict what a person will say and prepare some phrases that are easy for you to remember and pronounce. Did your interviewees use any similar language? What patterns did you notice?

2. Did you notice if anyone answered using modals (should, could, must)? How would this change the advice?

3. Was their advice what you expected? Who got the best advice for each question? Share answers and choose one for your group. Share the best advice for each question with the other groups.

Part 2: Giving Advice

Discussion Starter

- Who asks you for advice? About what?

- Who do you ask when you need:

  o Medical advice

  o Legal advice

  o Academic advice

  o Personal advice (about friends or relationships)

- Who has given you the best advice? Share a story about what the situation was and the advice you received.

Language Lesson: Giving Advice

Modals are often used when giving advice. *Should* is one of the most common modals.

> You *should* study two hours every night.

What You Learned	*What Is More Common*
Ought to and *Had better*. These are still used occasionally, but *should* is used most of the time. *You ought to take care of your parents when they get older.* [moral obligations] *You had better have your car inspected annually.* [or else something negative will happen]	*Should* is used for all of these situations. *You should study two hours every night* *You should take care of your parents when they get older.* *You should have your car inspected annually.* *Should* can also be used in the negative. *You should not eat so much sugar.* *Could* is another popular modal to use when giving advice. It is considered less strong than should and is sometimes used when there is more than one suggestion. *What should I do to get a better grade in Bio 101?* *You could buy the study guide. You could also visit the TA.*

Other common ways to give advice include

I suggest/recommend	My recommendation is . . .
You might try . . .	I guess I would
You might want to . . .	I think you could . . .
If it were me . . .	If I were you . . .
I would . . .	Could you (phrase it in the form of a question)
How about . . .	
Why don't you . . .	Could you schedule time in the lab for extra practice?
You could/should . . .	

Notice that using these common phrases sounds more like **hedging** or softening. They don't sound as forceful. Which do you think are more formal? Less formal?

Using the Imperative

Sometimes people will use an **imperative** and then the *–ing* form of a verb to give advice. This might seem stronger. You can soften them by adding one of the phrases in the previous list.

Start doing your homework.

Softer: You might want to start doing your homework.

Consider skipping the party and studying instead.

Softer: You could consider skipping the party. . . .

Try taking a multivitamin.

Stop drinking so much.

Note: In the end, it is very important to notice who is giving the advice. Just because a professor says uses the word *should* in *You should reread the chapter*, doesn't mean it's an option for you to not do that. He or she is really telling you what to do and is not offering advice.

Pronunciation Note: *Should* can be and often is contracted in spoken English.

You *shouldn't* eat so much sugar.

If you use *had better* or *had better not*, it is also contracted.

He'd better get more sleep.

He'd better not miss any more classes.

PRACTICE 1: PRONUNCIATION

How does each of these phrase really sound?

Phrase	Pronunciation
You might want to . . .	
You ought to . . .	
You had better . . .	
How about . . .	
Why don't you . . .	
I would . . .	
. . . could have . . .	
. . . should have . . .	
. . . would have . . .	
Could you . . .	
I sort of think you could have . . .	

PRACTICE 2: USING THE LANGUAGE

Read this list of things to do in case of an earthquake. Choose one point from each section (before, during, and after) and rewrite it so that it contains advice language.

Earthquakes

Earthquakes are sudden rolling or shaking events caused by movement under the earth's surface. Earthquakes happen along cracks in the earth's surface, called fault lines, and can be felt over large areas, although they usually last less than one minute. Earthquakes cannot be predicted—although scientists are working on it!

All 50 states and 5 U.S. territories are at some risk for earthquakes. Earthquakes can happen at any time of the year.

Before an Earthquake

- Look around places where you spend time. Identify safe places such as under a sturdy piece of furniture or against an interior wall in your home, office or school so that when the shaking starts, you Drop to the ground, Cover your head and neck with your arms, and if a safer place is nearby, crawl to it and Hold On.

- Practice how to **"Drop, Cover, and Hold On!"**

  o To react quickly you must practice often. You may only have seconds to protect yourself in an earthquake.

- Before an earthquake occurs, secure items that could fall and cause injuries (e.g., bookshelves, mirrors, light fixtures).

- Store critical supplies (e.g., water, medication) and documents.

- Plan how you will communicate with family members, including multiple methods by making a family emergency communication plan.

- When choosing your home or business, check if the building is earthquake resistant per local building codes.

During an Earthquake

If you are inside a building:

- Stay where you are until the shaking stops. Do not run outside. Do not get in a doorway as this does not provide protection from falling or flying objects, and you may not be able to remain standing.

- Drop down onto your hands and knees so the earthquake doesn't knock you down. Drop to the ground (before the earthquake drops you!)

- Cover your head and neck with your arms to protect yourself from falling debris.

  o If you are in danger from falling objects, and you can move safely, crawl for additional cover under a sturdy desk or table.

  o If there is low furniture or an interior wall or corner nearby, and the path is clear, these may also provide some additional cover.

  o Stay away from glass, windows, outside doors and walls, and anything that could fall, such as light fixtures or furniture.

- Hold on to any sturdy covering so you can move with it until the shaking stops. Stay where you are until the shaking stops.

If getting safely to the floor to take cover won't be possible:

- Identify an inside corner of the room away from windows and objects that could fall on you. The Earthquake Country Alliance advises getting as low as possible to the floor. People who use wheelchairs or other mobility devices should lock their wheels and remain seated until the shaking stops. Protect your head and neck with your arms, a pillow, a book, or whatever is available.

If you are in bed when you feel the shaking:

- If you are in bed: Stay there and cover your head and neck with a pillow. At night, hazards and debris are difficult to see and avoid; attempts to move in the dark result in more injuries than remaining in bed.

If you are outside when you feel the shaking:

- If you are outdoors when the shaking starts, move away from buildings, streetlights, and utility wires. Once in the open, "Drop, Cover, and Hold On." Stay there until the shaking stops. This might not be possible in a city, so you may need to duck inside a building to avoid falling debris.

If you are in a moving vehicle when you feel the shaking:

- If you are in a moving vehicle, stop as quickly and safely as possible and stay in the vehicle. Avoid stopping near or under buildings, trees, overpasses, and utility wires. Proceed cautiously once the earthquake has stopped. Avoid roads, bridges, or ramps that the earthquake may have damaged.

After an Earthquake

- When the shaking stops, look around. If there is a clear path to safety, leave the building and go to an open space away from damaged areas.

- If you are trapped, do not move about or kick up dust.

- If you have a cell phone with you, use it to call or text for help.

- Tap on a pipe or wall or use a whistle, if you have one, so that rescuers can locate you.

- Once safe, monitor local news reports via battery operated radio, TV, social media, and cell phone text alerts for emergency information and instructions.

- Be prepared to "Drop, Cover, and Hold on" in the likely event of aftershocks.

From: Official website of the Department of Homeland Security: https://www.ready.gov/earthquakes.

PRACTICE 3: GIVING ADVICE

Work with a partner. Give one piece of advice for each situation.

1. a friend needs a hotel recommendation for his visit to your school

   Advice: _____

2. a tourist wants to know what to see on campus

   Advice: _____

3. a classmate wants to know how to improve his English

   Advice: _____

4. a friend is losing her financial support from her parents for tuition

   Advice: _____

5. a friend wants to quit smoking

   Advice: _____

6. your friend is suffering from allergies

   Advice: _____

7. a librarian about how to find a journal article

   Advice: _____

8. one of your research group members wants to buy a car

   Advice: _____

PRACTICE 4: ROLE-PLAYS

Work with a partner. Your teacher will assign you roles. Everyone will develop the role-play for the same situation. Be prepared to present your role-play and notice how the ideas and language differ.

Many students gain a lot of weight when they first go away to college. It is sometimes called the Freshman 15. Think about why this happens. When a friend comes to you and asks what to do since gaining so much weight, offer some advice.

Participants—

Group A: friend to friend

Group B: patient to doctor or nurse at the health center

Group C: student to freshman advisor

Group D: student to parent

Get Acquainted

Advice columns are in many news sources and websites. Two of the most popular are Dear Abby and Dear Ann. Find two letters that you find interesting. Summarize the problem in Column 1. Then ask a classmate for their advice and complete Column 2. Ask someone born in the United States for their advice and put that in Column 3. Finally, copy the expert's advice from the news source in Column 4.

Problem in Letter	Classmate's Advice	Advice from Someone Born in the U.S.	Expert's Advice
Letter 1			
Letter 2			

PRACTICE 5: ANALYSIS

Work with a group. Compare your Get Acquainted charts and answer these questions.

1. How did the advice change based on who was giving it?

2. What did you notice about the advice language people used?

3. Who gave the best advice?

Unit 6

Making Excuses and Giving Apologies

Part 1: Making Excuses

Discussion Starter

- What might be the reason or excuse you give for not finishing an assignment? For not accepting a party invitation? For being late?

- Describe a time when someone made an excuse to you. What was the situation? How did you feel?

- What are some situations for which you might need to make an excuse?

Language Lesson: Making Excuses

When do you need to give an excuse in English? There are three general categories:

- **Leaving** (a conversation or event; saying goodbye)

- **Apologizing** (for something you did or didn't do; saying I'm sorry)

- **Rejecting** (an invitation, a request for help; explaining why you can't do something)

Making excuses often follows a two-part format.

Category	Part 1	Part 2
Leaving	A reason or excuse (to avoid being abrupt or impolite) + . . .	some form of *goodbye*
Apologizing	Some form of *I'm sorry* + . . .	a reason or excuse (to explain why you are apologizing)
Rejecting	Some form of *no* + . . .	a reason or excuse (to avoid hurting the other person)

Examples:

> Wow. I can't believe how late it is. I have a long day tomorrow. I'll talk to you later.

> I am so sorry I'm late. My car wouldn't start and I had to wait for the tow truck to come.

> I wish I could hang out, but I have a huge midterm tomorrow and I need to study.

Note: Apologizing can add a third component: an offer to compensate.

> I'm so sorry I broke your mug. I wasn't expecting the coffee to be so hot and I dropped it. I'll buy you another one.

PRACTICE 1: UNEXPECTED ANSWERS

Some language that you hear after you make an excuse might seem unexpected, but these words and phrases are expected or more common to a native speaker. Read each phrase and use the blank to try to guess what the person might say.

Dialogue 1

1: Hey, want to go to dinner on Friday?

2: Oh, I can't. I already have plans.

1: What are you doing?

2: _____

1: You can do that anytime. You should come with us.

2: _____

Dialogue 2

1: You're late to work again.

2: Sorry. My car broke down.

1: Why don't you get it fixed?

2: _____

Dialogue 3

1: Want another drink?

2: No, I'm thinking about heading out.

1: You can't go now. You just got here. It's still early.

2: Sorry, but I'm actually not feeling that well.

1: What's bothering you? I have some aspirin in my bag.

2: _____

PRACTICE 2: GOOD REASONS

Whenever possible, it's good if you can have a good reason for why you are leaving, apologizing, or rejecting. Look at each situation and think of good excuses.

1. Reason to be late for work (to a boss):

   _____

2. Reason to be late for class (to a professor):

   _____

3. Reason for a late assignment (to a professor):

   _____

4. Reason for speeding (to a police officer):

   _____

5. Reason for being late for dinner (to a friend):

   _____

6. Reason for being late to pick someone up (to a date):

   _____

7. Reason for losing a book you borrowed (to a classmate):

   _____

8. Reason for staining a sweater you borrowed (to a roommate):

   _____

Part 2: Giving Apologies

Discussion Starter

- What are some reasons you might have to apologize?

- How do you apologize? Are there certain words or phrases to use?

- What would you say in each of these situations:

  o You lost the sweater you borrowed from your roommate.

  o You need to tell a professor why you didn't complete the homework assignment on time.

  o You forgot to call your mom on her birthday.

  o You are late to an appointment at the student healthcare center.

  o You need to borrow a pencil from a classmate.

  o You broke a mug at a friend's apartment.

  o You need to answer a phone while you are talking to someone else (in person).

  o You need to interupt someone during a group discussion.

- What are some other situations in which you might need to apologize?

Language Lesson: *I'm sorry* or *Excuse Me*

I'm sorry or *Sorry* is commonly associated with apologies. Note that longer is more formal, so *Sorry* is a little less formal. It can also be emphasized by adding a word before it: *I'm so sorry. So sorry!. I'm really/very sorry. Excuse me* is often used when you need someone to move out of your way. These phrases have many other uses as well and are commonly confused.

Use *I'm sorry* when:

- you forget someone's name or don't know their name: I'm sorry, I forgot your name.

- you hurt someone's feelings: I'm sorry, I didn't mean that.

- you hurt someone physically: I'm sorry. I stepped on your toe. You okay?

- you need someone to repeat something: I'm sorry, can you say that again?

- you interrupt (less formal): I'm sorry. I'd rather go see an action movie.

- you said something wrong: I'm sorry. That's not what I meant. I meant. . . .

- you reject an invitation: I'm sorry. I already have plans for Friday night.

- you want to express sympathy about an illness or death: I'm sorry to hear about your grandmother.

- you want to express sympathy about a situation: I'm sorry you lost your job.

- you are late: I'm sorry I'm late. Traffic was terrible.

- you have bad news: I'm sorry to say this, but you failed the midterm.

- you lose something: I'm sorry I lost your book. I'll buy you a new copy.

- you can't help someone who asked for help: I'm so sorry. I'm going to be late for class. I can try to help you later though.

Use *Excuse me* when:

- you need a favor or information: Excuse me, can you tell me where the bathroom is?

- you cough, clear your throat, or sneeze: [Sneeze]. Excuse me. My allergies are acting up.

- you want to get someone's attention: Excuse me, I think we're ready to order.

- you interrupt politely (more formal): Excuse me, but I need to interrupt.

- you leave a room, group, conversation: Excuse me. I need to go make a quick call.

- you need someone to move out of your way: Excuse me. Can I get through here?

- you want to be more formal: Excuse me. I'd like to add to the point you were making.

  Note: *Hey* is a very informal way for friends to say *Excuse me*.

  Hey. We're over here.

PRACTICE 3: *I'M SORRY* OR *EXCUSE ME*?

Work with a partner. Decide if you should use *I'm sorry* (S) or *Excuse me* (E) in each situation. Are there any situations in which you might hear both phrases?

1. _____ You don't know someone's name and you need to introduce him/her.

2. _____ You don't have any money to lend your roommate.

3. _____ You want your significant other to stop looking at their cell phone during a conversation.

4. _____ You are the TA and the students won't stop talking.

5. _____ You want someone to tell you the time.

6. _____ You are talking to someone but you need to answer your cell phone.

7. _____ You need to get off the train at the next stop and someone is standing at the door.

8. _____ You need the clerk to tell you if they have any of the sweatshirts in an XL.

9. _____ You forgot to bring the notes that you promised to lend a classmate.

10. _____ You spill coffee on the table while having dinner at a friend's house.

11. _____ Your friend gets upset after you've said you don't like her new haircut.

12. _____ Your friend tells you that her father is in the hospital.

Language Lesson: Getting Clarification

Sometimes native speakers don't use *Excuse me* or *I'm sorry* when they don't understand, but they do try to clarify the words or information by repeating part of what they said so that the speaker can then fill in the part the listener missed. In other words, repeat what you did understand and ask for clarification about what you missed.

Example:

For tomorrow's class, you'll need to read the chapter on artificial intelligence so we can discuss the benefits.

You hear:

For tomorrow's class, you'll need to read the chapter on artificial intelligence so we can discuss [MISSED INFORMATION].

You ask:

For tomorrow's class, we need to read the chapter on artificial intelligence so we can discuss what?

Or You ask:

I'm sorry, what did you say we will discuss?

PRACTICE 4: GETTING CLARIFICATION

Read each statement that you might hear in class. Write a question to get clarification of the missed information.

1. <u>You hear</u>: For tomorrow's class, you'll need to [MISSED INFORMATION] on artificial intelligence so we can discuss the benefits.

   You ask: _____

2. <u>You hear</u>: For tomorrow's class, you'll need to read the chapter [MISSED INFORMATION] so we can discuss the benefits.

   You ask: _____

3. <u>You hear</u>: For [MISSING INFORMATION], you'll need to read the chapter on artificial intelligence so we can discuss the benefits.

   You ask: _____

4. <u>You hear</u>: For tomorrow's class, you'll need to read the chapter on artificial intelligence [MISSED INFORMATION] the benefits.

   You ask: _____

Get Acquainted

Choose someplace you visit regularly or are interested in learning more about. Observe the location for one hour. Listen for instances of *Excuse me* or *I'm sorry* and making excuses in general. Write a report with five observations about the wording, the responses, and the factors that may or may not affect the interaction.

> *Example:* Location: Store at the mall
>
> When a woman wanted to return something, she made an excuse about the size: She said "I'd likie to exchange this. I need a smaller size."
>
> When a clerk didn't notice a shopper, the shopper said "Excuse me. Can you tell me if you have any more of these in the back room."

PRACTICE 4: ANALYSIS

Work with a group. Compare your reports.

1. In many cases, English is formulaic. You can predict what a person will say and prepare some phrases that are easy for you to remember and pronounce. Did people use I'm sorry and Excuse me the way you were expecting?

2. What kind of excuses did they give? What were the situations? Do you think these were good excuses? How would you feel if these were given to you? Did tone of voice make a difference? In other words, did the words sound genuine?

3. What notes do you have about each interaction about age, gender, or time and location? Did these affect the interactions? Did this affect the patterns you noticed?

Unit 7

Invitations and Thank-Yous

Part 1: Extending, Rejecting, and Accepting Invitations

Discussion Starter

- What invitations have you received recently? What were the details: event, location, time?

- What kind of information does an invitation need to include?

- Why might you accept or turn down an invitation?

Language Lesson: Invitations

There are many ways **to extend an invitation**. Some are very formal, but many sound less formal.

What You Learned	What Is More Common
I'd like to invite you to . . .	How about [coming, going, joining me . . .]?

Other phrases are:

Let's go . . .

How'd you like to . . .

Do you want to (wanna) . . .

Hey, we're going to/doing . . . Want to come/join us?

I wanted to know if you want to/would like to . . .

Would you like to . . .

There's a [party] Friday night. Wanna go?

After receiving an invitation, you can **accept** it.

What You Learned	*What Is More Common*
Thank you. That sounds nice. I would be happy to come.	Sounds great.

Other phrases are:

Yes, Yeah, Sure, Ok (or some form of positive acceptance).

That sounds great/good/like fun.

I'd love that.

Why not?

Here are some common ways to **reject** an invitation.

What You Learned	*What Is More Common*
Thank you for the invitation, but I am sorry I cannot attend.	I can't. I've gotta. . . . Sorry. Can't. Gotta. . . .

Notice that you can also add an apology and reason or excuse. Review Making Excuses in Unit 6.

I wish I could, but. . . .

I'd like to, but. . . .

I'm sorry, I can't. I already have plans.

I can't make it. I am going to be out of town.

I'm busy then. Maybe some other time.

Thanks, but I can't. I have a huge test the next day and I need to study.

It is possible to give a tentative answer:

Can I let you know? I need to check with my [significant other].

I'm not sure. I may have to work. I need to check my schedule.

Oh, I really shouldn't . . .

PRACTICE 1: DISCUSSION

Answer these questions with a partner or small group.

1. What information does the invitee need to know (example: time)? When does this information need to be provided?

2. What are good excuses for turning down an invitation?

3. In your country, what determines who pays for the event? Does it matter what type of event it is or who is attending? Talk about the circumstances.

4. What is common etiquette when invited to someone's home? Does the etiquette change based on the reason for the invitation?

5. Have you been to any American social events? How are they the same as and different from similar events in your country?

6. What do you bring to each event? Who pays? What time do you arrive if each event is listed as beginning at 7 PM?

birthday party

dinner at your advisor's house

potluck dinner

dinner at a friend's house

graduation party

baby shower

bridal shower

bachelor/bachelorette party

business lunch

date

wedding

job interview

happy hour with other students from your department

department picnic

PRACTICE 2: GROUP DISCUSSION

Work with a partner to plan a dinner party. Consider these factors:

- Because you are having the party in campus housing, there is limited space and you can only invite eight people.
- You can invite anyone you want—famous people or personal guests (or a combination), living people or historical figures (even if they are no longer living).
- Decide who will sit where at the table. Remember to include a place for yourself.
- Make sure to consider the factors such as age, gender, status, and personality.
- Also decide what you will serve (food and drinks), if there will be party favors, and what the entertainment will be.
- Consider having a theme for your party.

Guests and Seating Arrangement:

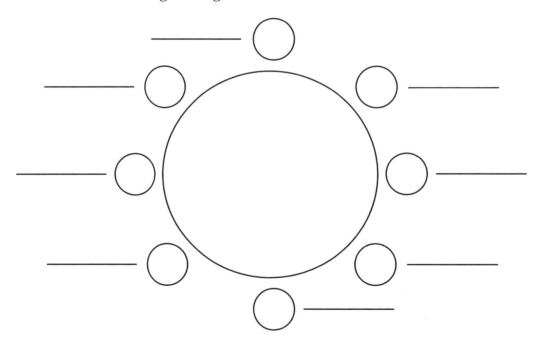

Reasons for guests and seating:

_____

_____

_____

Food and drinks:

_____

_____

_____

Theme:

_____

_____

_____

Other details:

_____

_____

_____

PRACTICE 3: COMMON RESPONSES

Match the common language you might hear in a discussion about an invitation (on the left) with a response (on the right).

____ 1. What can I bring?

a. Just yourself.

____ 2. What time works for you?

b. Thanks for having me.

____ 3. Wanna have a drink to celebrate finals being over?

c. Sounds like fun.

____ 4. Where should we meet?

d. Six is good. Or That'll work.

____ 5. How about Saturday night?

e. Any one is fine. I don't care. I'm flexible.

____ 6. Meet you there at 6.

f. I know Michael's. Let's go there.

____ 7. You didn't need to bring anything.

g. I wanted to.

____ 8. Thanks for coming.

h. Say 5ish?

____ 9. Which movie do you want to see?

i. That works.

Part 2: Expressing Thanks

Discussion Starter

- What are the different ways people have thanked you for something?

- What language have you used to thank people for doing something for you or for helping you?

Language Lesson: Expressing Thanks

The most common way to express thanks to an invitation (or in other contexts) is to simply say *Thanks*.

What You Probably Learned	What Is More Common
Thank you. That is so nice of you.	Thanks.

Other ways to express thanks:

I owe you.	I can't thank you enough.
You're a lifesaver.	Appreciate the [help].
I don't know how to thank you.	Thanks. Thanks a lot. Thanks so much. Thanks a million.

Expressing thanks when you are not expecting something or didn't ask for something:

That's a nice surprise. Thanks.

I didn't expect that. Thanks.

You read my mind! Thanks.

You shouldn't have.

You didn't need to do that.

Expressing thanks for a business or academic meeting (with a boss or professor):

Thanks for your time.

Thanks for meeting with me.

Thanks for a failed attempt:

Thanks for trying.

Appreciate the time/help/effort anyway.

Thanks anyway.

Thanks for trying at least.

Here are some ways to respond:

What You Probably Learned	What Is More Common
You're welcome. Or My pleasure.	No problem.
	You bet.
	That's all right.
	Don't mention it.
	Not at all.
	It was nothing.
	No worries.
	You got it.

Get Acquainted

Make five offers (example: a piece of gum). Complete the chart.

Item Offered	To Whom	Invitation Language	Response	Details about the Interaction and Tone of Voice

PRACTICE 4: ANALYSIS

Work with a group. Compare your reports.

1. What language did people use to respond? What were their excuses for accepting or rejecting?

2. In many cases, English is formulaic. You can predict what a person will say and prepare some phrases that are easy for you to remember and pronounce. Did any of you offer similar things? Do you see any patterns?

3. How did you choose to respond to their expressions of thanks? How was each person's tone of voice when they responded to your invitation?

4. What details of the interaction might have affected the communication? In other words, do you think location or gender might have changed the responses?

Unit 8

Complimenting and Complaining

Part 1: Complimenting

Discussion Starter

- What can you compliment? What should you not compliment? Why?

- Who can you compliment? Who should you not compliment? What makes the difference?

- What was the last thing someone complimented you on? How did it make you feel?

- What was the last compliment you gave? How did the person respond?

Language Lesson: Complimenting

A **compliment** is an expression of praise or admiration that you give to someone else. Compliments usually make the receiver feel good, but they also make the giver happy. Compliments play a part in social, academic, and professional settings, so it is important to understand the wording and patterns associated with them.

It is important to not make the compliments too personal. Think about age, gender, status, and the other factors that affect communication when deciding who and what to compliment. Tone of voice is very important. You don't want to sound too personal in a professional setting.

Examples:

You look nice today.

You have pretty eyes.

I like your [necklace].

You play the piano so well.

Those shoes are great.

Your research paper was great.

Most compliments fall into four general categories.

1. Looks (physical appearance)

2. Skills (talents, things someone does well)

3. Accomplishments (work someone has done successfully)

4. Tangible Items (things a person owns or has)

When you receive a compliment, you must respond:

What You Probably Learned	What Is More Common
Thank you. That's so nice.	Thanks.
Thank you for saying so.	

Ways to thank someone and/or disagree (reject the compliment)

I like your shirt.

Really? This is so old! Or I got this for only five bucks on a clearance rack.

Thanks + Returned Compliment

I like your shirt.

Thanks. I like yours, too.

Or, I like your [SOMETHING ELSE if they don't have the same item].

Pronunciation Note: Compliments are meant to be genuine, so it is helpful to both follow the pattern and use an appreciative tone of voice. Even when you're rejecting the compliment, the tone of voice should be grateful.

When someone is "fishing" for a compliment, they ask a question like, *Do you like my new shirt?* or *What do you think about my new shirt?* Or, they might make a statement such as *I'm not sure I like this new shirt I bought.*

Since you have not chosen to give the compliment, it can be challenging to make it genuine.

Strategy: Give a general compliment:

Do you like my new sweater?

It looks warm!

Sometimes friends or family ask you what you think and you don't want to lie, but you also don't want to hurt their feelings.

Strategy: Give a truthful statement:

Do you like my new shirt?

I do like the new shirt, but I actually like the one you wore yesterday better.

PRACTICE 1: IMPROVE THE RESPONSES

Read each compliment and rejection. Then write a better rejection phrase.

Dialogue 1

Compliment: You look great today.

Rejection: Oh, I don't. I look awful.

Better rejection: _____

Dialogue 2

Compliment: Love your shoes.

Rejection: These are so old. They're ready for the trash.

Better rejection: _____

Dialogue 3

Compliment: That's a pretty dress. Where did you get it?

Rejection: You're kidding. My mom got this for me. She doesn't have the same taste as me.

Better rejection: _____

Dialogue 4

Compliment: Congratulations. You gave a great speech today in class. I wish I spoke as well as you.

Rejection: No way. I'm not good at all.

Better rejection: _____

Dialogue 5

Compliment: Your writing is really improving in my class.

Rejection: I'm still not good enough.

Better rejection: _____

PRACTICE 2: GIVING GENUINE COMPLIMENTS

You need your compliments to sound genuine. Don't compliment someone if you don't mean it. And avoid flattery (compliments combined with requests): *You're a great writing teacher. Can you proofread my resume for me? I don't trust anyone else.* Write a compliment for each situation/item.

1. a friend's new car _____

2. a classmate's good oral presentation _____

3. a professor's lecture _____

4. a dinner host's cooking _____

5. a woman's hair _____

6. a peer's publication acceptance _____

7. a birthday present your roommate bought you _____

PRACTICE 3: AVOIDING UNACCEPTABLE QUESTIONS OR STATEMENTS

Part 1: Read each statement. Write A for Acceptable or U for Unacceptable.

1. I like your watch. How much did you pay for it? _____

2. Your new haircut makes you look older/younger. _____

3. That's a really bright blue shirt. _____

4. You look great. You should wear that color more often! _____

5. I wish I could wear that style. _____

6. Have you lost weight? _____

7. You are so good at English. _____

8. My mother has that same dress! _____

Part 2: Rewrite the unacceptable compliments and then write a response for all eight items.

_____

_____

_____

_____

Get Acquainted

Give five compliments. Complete the chart.

Compliment	Offered to Whom	Response	Details of the Interaction

PRACTICE 4: ANALYSIS

Work with a group. Compare your Get Acquainted charts and answer
these questions.

1. In many cases, English is formulaic. You can predict what a
   person will say and prepare some phrases that are easy for you
   to remember and pronounce. Look at the responses. Did people
   respond the way you expected? Did anyone reject or return the
   compliment?

2. What details might have affected the interaction. For example,
   do men and women react differently?

3. How did you feel when you were giving the compliments?
   Do you think this is a good way to start a conversation
   with someone? Are there any settings that are not ideal for
   compliments?

Part 2: Complaining

Discussion Starter

- What are some things people complain about? What do you complain about most?

- How do you feel when someone complains? Can you complain too much or too little?

- To whom do you usually complain? Would you ever complain to a stranger? Do you complain about different things to different people?

- Does complaining have a purpose?

Language Lesson: Complaining

Everyone complains sometimes. Common things that people complain about include:

weather	food
school or work	service
traffic	waiting in line
money	other people
time	

Consider the context. You complain differently to your boss than you do to your friend or a stranger (at a bus stop or in line at the store).

Consider the result. Complain in the hopes of finding a resolution.

Consider the tone. Complain "politely" rather than "whining" to get help finding a resolution.

Complaint + Request

Your paper is late. Please email it to me by the end of the day if you want to receive credit.

Complaint + Question

My mother is coming to visit. Do you mind if I stack up all your books and move them to your room?

Complaint + Request

My throat really hurts. Do you have anything I can take?

<u>Note:</u> Do not reject the person's ideas.

<u>Good:</u>

My throat really hurts. What can I do?

You should stop by the health center.

That's a good idea.

<u>Not So Good:</u>

My throat really hurts.

You should stop by the health center.

I don't have the money to pay for a doctor!

Indirect Complaint

Let's go to the Union to grab some dinner.

I can't. I really have to keep studying.

You've been studying for three hours already.

Well, my midterm is tomorrow.

Dinner is only served until 8. Maybe you can take a short break and then come right back and finish studying.

Okay. Maybe you're right. I'll take a break. Gotta eat, right?

Blame Something or Someone Else

I only tripped because these stupid shoelaces won't stay tied.

I didn't do as well on the test because my roommate had the television on too loud and I couldn't concentrate.

Offer a Reason

I think there has been a misunderstanding. I asked for the gluten-free pizza, but this one has regular crust.

Offer an Apology (even if it isn't your fault!)

I'm sorry, but I think you gave me the wrong change. I gave you a $20.

I'm sorry, but I don't think the heat in my hotel room is working.

Note: Expected responses include a reason or apology back.

You're right. I didn't hear you say gluten-free. Let me put a new order in.

I'm so sorry. I thought you gave me a $10.

I'm sorry. Let me send someone up to check on that for you.

PRACTICE 1: WORD CHOICE

Work with a partner. Improve these complaints.

Complaint	Improvement
[to a server at a restaurant] My hamburger is raw.	My hamburger is too rare for me. Can you please ask the chef to cook it a little longer?
[to your roommate] It's too hot in here.	
[to a professor] The due date is hard to make.	
[to a cashier at a store] This sweater has a hole in it.	
[to a lab mate] The lab report has too many mistakes.	
[to a ticket agent at the movie theatre] Can you hurry up?	
[to a friend who is making you late to class] Can you hurry up?	
[to a waiter who forgot something you ordered] I asked for a glass of water 20 minutes ago.	

PRACTICE 2: COMPLAINING

Write a complaint on these topics. Choose wording based on the person you are speaking to.

1. you don't have not enough time to finish a test

   To your friend

   _____

   To the professor

   _____

2. the shirt your brother sent you for your birthday

   To your roommate

   _____

   To your brother

   _____

3. the weather has been rainy for days

   To a friend

   _____

   To a colleague at the company where you are interning

   _____

4. you have a bad headache

    To your mom

    _____

    To a doctor

    _____

5. your friend is late all the time

    To the friend who is late

    _____

    To another friend

    _____

6. you had a bad meal at a restaurant

    To the person you are dating/friends with who invited you to the
    restaurant

    _____

    To the manager of the restaurant

    _____

PRACTICE 3: RESPONSES

Work with a partner. For each situation in Practice 2. Write a response you are likely to hear.

1.

2.

3.

4.

5.

6.

PRACTICE 4: ROLE-PLAYS

Work with a partner. Write a short dialogue for each of these situations. Prepare to perform it for the class.

1. You are two friends talking about a class you are taking. Complaints: amount of homework, early start time, hard teacher

2. You are talking to an apartment manager about possibly renting an apartment. Complaints: noisy neighbor, sink drips all the time, crack in the ceiling

3. You are talking to teammates about losing the soccer game. Complaints: new shoes were uncomfortable, bad field, one teammate (who is not there) didn't play well

4. You are talking to your former roommate on the phone about your new roommate. Complaints: slams the door all the time, cooks food that makes the apartment smell, tracks in mud

5. You are complaining to a flight agent at the airport. Complaints: delayed flight will cause you to miss your connection, lack of compensation for the inconvenience, infrequent updates as you wait in the gate area

Get Acquainted

Complete the restaurant evaluation form for a place you eat before the next class. You can compliment or complain using language from both parts of this unit.

We value your patronage. Let us know what you think.

Did you join us for: (circle one)   Breakfast   Lunch   Dinner

How many people were in your party: _____

Have you dined with us before? (circle one)   Yes   No

Rate the following items

5 = Excellent   4 = Good   3 = Average   2 = Below Average   1 = Poor

Food Quality   5   4   3   2   1

Comment: _____

Food Quantity   5   4   3   2   1

Comment: _____

Service   5   4   3   2   1

Comment: _____

Wait Time   5   4   3   2   1

Comment: _____

Atmosphere   5   4   3   2   1

Comment: _____

Price   5   4   3   2   1

Comment: _____

Cleanliness   5   4   3   2   1

Comment: _____

Restrooms   5   4   3   2   1   NA (Not applicable, Did not visit the restroom)

Comment: _____

Would you visit us again? (circle one)   Yes   No   Maybe

Reason: _____

PRACTICE 5: ANALYSIS

Work with a group. Compare your Get Acquainted charts and answer these questions.

1. What did you complain about? What wording did you use?

2. What did you compliment?

3. Did you share any of your complaints or compliments with the restaurant or the people you ate with?

4. Would you recommend this establishment? Why or why not?

Unit 9

Congratulations and Condolences

Part 1: Congratulations

Discussion Starter

- How do you define congratulations? How do you define condolences?

- What is the most recent thing you did for which someone congratulated you or something someone else did for which you offered your congratulations?

Language Lesson: Congratulations

There are several ways you can congratulate someone.

Congratulations.	Bravo.
Kudos.	Way to go.
Cheers, or Hear, Hear. [Usually toasting someone over drinks]	You rule/rock.
	Good/Great job.
Hats off.	Awesome.
Best wishes.	

You can sometimes use compliments and congratulations interchangeably. Review Unit 8 and compliments.

Example:

Congratulations. Your speech in class was awesome.

Well done.

Nice job on that report you wrote about the company project.

You really went to town on this meal. It tastes great.

Pronunciation Note: To emphasize a point, native speakers may stretch a word or phrase.

Niiiiiice job!

It tastes greaaaat!

Part 2: Condolences

Discussion Starter

- What is a recent event for which someone offered their condolences to you or for which you offered your condolences?

- Can you think of a situation in which both congratulations and condolences might be offered? What factors, such as culture, age, or gender, might determine whether a situation warrants congratulations or condolences?

Language Lesson: Condolences

There are several ways you can offer condolences.

I'm [so] sorry.	I'm here for you.
You have my sympathy.	I'm here if you want to talk.
I [can] commiserate with you.	I feel for you.
I wish I could make you feel better.	I know how you feel.
	This must be so hard for you.
My thoughts and prayers are with you.	

Offering condolences can be very hard depending on the situation because you might not know how to make the person feel better (for example, when someone passes away). In some cases, you can simply say you don't know what to say or you can offer to help. Your tone of voice should always be sincere.

I don't know what to say.

I can't imagine what you're going through.

I know what you're going through/how you feel.

I wish there was something I could do.

Let me know if there is anything I can do.

Do you need me to do anything at all?

Is there anything at all that I can do?/Can I do anything?

PRACTICE 1: SITUATIONS

For each situation, decide if it is usually congratulations or condolences.

1. birthday _____

2. anniversary _____

3. engagement _____

4. wedding _____

5. pregnancy _____

6. new baby _____

7. new job _____

8. lost job _____

9. death _____

10. promotion _____

11. accident _____

12. retirement _____

13. graduation _____

14. new car _____

15. election win _____

16. election loss _____

17. divorce _____

18. break up with boyfriend/girlfriend _____

PRACTICE 2: AMBIGUOUS—COULD IT BE THE OPPOSITE?

Choose five situations from Practice 1 (p. 144). Write a situation or factor that would require the opposite reaction of what is more common or—not necessarily congratulations or condolences.

1.

2.

3.

4.

5.

PRACTICE 3: DIALOGUE COMPLETION

Work with a partner. Try to guess what the common response is and write a common way to extend the conversation.

1. I'm pregnant./My wife is pregnant. _____

_____

2. I had a car accident. _____

_____

3. I got engaged. _____

_____

4. I'm graduating. _____

_____

5. My grandmother passed away. _____

_____

6. It's my birthday. _____

_____

7. I got laid off from my job. _____

_____

8. I failed my math test. _____

_____

9. I had a fight with my boyfriend/girlfriend. _____

_____

10. I got an article published. _____

_____

11. My advisor is leaving the university. _____

_____

12. I'm moving to [NEW CITY/COUNTRY]. _____

_____

Get Acquainted

Choose a television show (or shows) to watch. Listen for instances of congratulations or condolences. Write details about the instances. Notice the wording, the responses, and the factors that may or may not affect the interaction. You might also be able to find scripts online or use a corpus to find more authentic examples. If you use a written script, highlight or underline stressed syllables and words and write how it will sound in English (not how it is supposed to sound). (See the Appendix.)

PRACTICE 4: ANALYSIS

Work with a group. Compare your reports.

1. Did people use congratulations and condolences the way you were expecting?

2. In many cases, English is formulaic. You can predict what a person will say and prepare some phrases that are easy for you to remember and pronounce. What kind of wording did they use? What were the situations and responses? Do you think these were common? How would you feel if these were given to you?

3. What notes do you have about each interaction about age, gender, or time and location? Did these affect the interactions? Did this affect the patterns you noticed?

Unit 10

Small Talk

Discussion Starter

- What do you talk about . . .

  o with a classmate the five minutes before class starts?

  o with a friend at a party?

  o with a stranger while standing in line at a store or restaurant?

  o with a neighbor on a bus taking you home for the day?

- Do you like small talk? Why or why not?

- Is small talk common in your country? How is it similar to or different from what you have noticed or know about small talk in English?

- What makes small talk challenging in English?

- When, where, and with whom is it appropriate? Inappropriate?

Language Lesson: Small Talk

When participating in small talk, both parties are expected to participate. One person is not more responsible than another to keep the conversation moving. It is important to be an active listener.

Strategies to Keep the Conversation Going/Give Encouragement to the Other Speaker

Ask *wh–* questions

Where are you from?

Ask for details

Do you like it here?

Give extended answers

1: Do you like it here?

2: Yes. I love how friendly everyone is and there are so many great restaurants!

Use body language

Eye contact, facial expressions, posture, gestures

Give verbal responses

1: So, I walk into class late.

2: Go on . . .

Use tag questions

1: I was late to class.

2: You were?

Repeat part of what the person said

1: I was late to class.

2: Late?

Ask more questions.

1: I was late to class.	2: Why?
1: I was late to class.	2: What happened?
1: I was late to class.	2: What did the teacher say?
1: I was late to class.	2: How late?

PRACTICE 1: SMALL TALK TOPICS

Make a list of small talk topics that you can use and another list of those you should avoid.

Use	Avoid
1.	1.
2.	2.
3.	3.
4.	4.
5.	5.
6.	6.
7.	7.
8.	8.
9.	9.
10.	10.

PRACTICE 2: APPROPRIATENESS

Work with a partner. Decide if each topic is appropriate (A) or inappropriate (I) to ask about to extend small talk.

1. Age _____

2. Where you live _____

3. Salary _____

4. Relationship status _____

5. Weight _____

6. What you do (job) _____

7. Major _____

8. Children _____

9. Family _____

10. Hometown _____

11. Religion _____

12. Rent _____

Go through the list again and think about if it could also be the opposite answer based on word choice, tone of voice, or other factors (such as gender or status) makes a difference. For example, asking about age is usually considered inappropriate. However, if you ask young children, they are often excited or proud to tell you they are 10 years old.

PRACTICE 3: WHAT DO YOU DO WHEN?

Work with a partner. Write an appropriate thing to say for each situation. Note that there are several ways to address each of these situations.

What do you say when:

1 you didn't hear the person (it is noisy) _____

2 you didn't hear the person (they were too quiet) _____

3 the person talks too fast _____

4 you didn't understand some words _____

5 you want them to clarify something they said _____

6 you need them to repeat something _____

7 you didn't understand a word _____

8 the person has an accent you don't understand _____

9 you want to clarify something they said (test your own comprehension) _____

10 the person asks if you understand (and you do) _____

    or the person asks if you understand (and you don't) _____

PRACTICE 4: DISCUSSION QUESTIONS

Work with a small group. Discuss these situations.

1. You see someone at a party that you want to meet. How do you approach the person? What do you talk about and not talk about?

2. Two interns see each other at work on Monday morning at the coffee machine after a three-day weekend. What should they talk about?

3. You see a professor first thing in the morning. What do you do?

4. The bus to campus is very crowded and you are forced to sit with someone you don't know. How do you start a conversation?

5. You want to study at the café, but it is crowded. How do you ask someone if you can sit at their table?

6. You've just been put into a group with three classmates you don't know. How do you get to know each other?

7. Your friend just got a new job. What do you say?

PRACTICE 5: EXTENDING CONVERSATIONS

Write a longer answer to these common small talk yes/no or one-word answer questions.

1. Do you like it here? _____

_____

2. Are you a student here? _____

_____

3. Do you like to travel? _____

_____

4. Do you like to go to the movies? _____

_____

5. Did you see the [baseball] game last night? _____

_____

6. Did you finish the homework yet? _____

_____

7. Have you been to New York? _____

_____

8. Do you have a job? _____

_____

9. Do you want to stay here or go home after graduation? _____

   _____

10. Do you want to live in a big city or a small town? _____

    _____

11. How many classes are you taking? _____

    _____

12. What time do you get up in the morning? _____

    _____

PRACTICE 6: ROLE-PLAYS

Work with a partner. Choose one situation from Practice 3 and write a dialogue extending the conversation. Be prepared to read your dialogue to the rest of the class. For your dialogue, highlight or underline stressed syllables and words and write how it will sound in English (not how it is supposed to sound). (See the Appendix.)

_____

_____

_____

_____

_____

_____

_____

_____

_____

_____

Get Acquainted

Part 1

Interview someone born in the United States. Explain that you are working on a project for your speaking class and would like to ask a few questions. Take notes on the answers.

1. The last time you made small talk with someone, where were you?

2. What was the context?

3. What did you talk about?

4. What is your favorite small talk topic?

Part 2

Participate in small talk with someone born in the United States. This can be someone you know or someone you just met. Use the strategies from this unit or any other units in your conversation. Prepare an oral report covering this content:

- who you talked to

- when the conversation took place

- where the conversation took place

- what you talked about

- the strategies you used

- the strategies they used

- if the person seemed interested (how did they show it) or not interested (draw a conclusion as to why)

PRACTICE 7: ANALYSIS

After everyone reports on their small talk experiences, answer these questions with a group.

1. What strategies seem to the most effective? Why?

2. What topics are the most common?

3. What factors might affect a conversation?

APPENDIX

Pronunciation-related material that may be useful.

- **Stress:** emphasized or prominence given to a certain syllable in a word or a certain word or phrase in a sentence

Note that the word that is stressed can dramatically change the meaning of a sentence (capping indicates the stressed word):

I didn't say you were stupid (Someone else did.)

I DIDN'T say you were stupid (I said something else.)

I didn't SAY you were stupid (I thought it.)

I didn't say YOU were stupid (I said someone else was.)

I didn't say you WERE stupid (I think you still are.)

I didn't say you were STUPID (I said you were something else.)

I didn't say you were STUPID (I said you were STUDIOUS).

- **Thought Groups:** groups of words that together form a meaning (*the pronunciation/of English/can be challenging*)

- **Linking:** letters or words that are connected (*Should I* sounds like *shouldeye*)

- **Pitch:** rise and fall of the voice

  o **Higher pitch:** usually used for positive statements; usually associated with submission, politeness, or friendliness

  o **Lower pitch:** usually used for negative statements; usually associated with dominance, confidence, or aggressiveness

- **Tone:** expresses a speaker's attitude; conveys meaning beyond words

- **Stretching:** emphasizes a word (*I'm reallllly sorry. I'm sooooo sorry.*)